This
Read, Listen, & Wonder
book belongs to:

CANDLEWICK PRESS

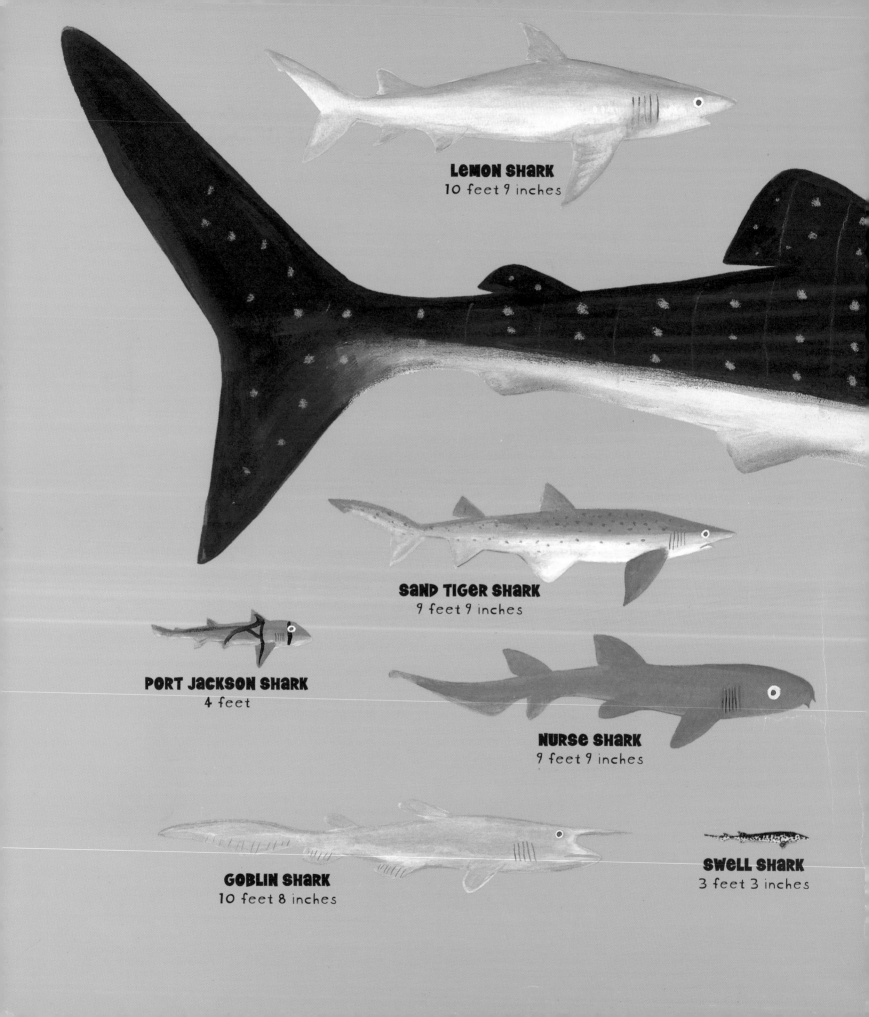

LEMON SHARK
10 feet 9 inches

SAND TIGER SHARK
9 feet 9 inches

PORT JACKSON SHARK
4 feet

NURSE SHARK
9 feet 9 inches

GOBLIN SHARK
10 feet 8 inches

SWELL SHARK
3 feet 3 inches

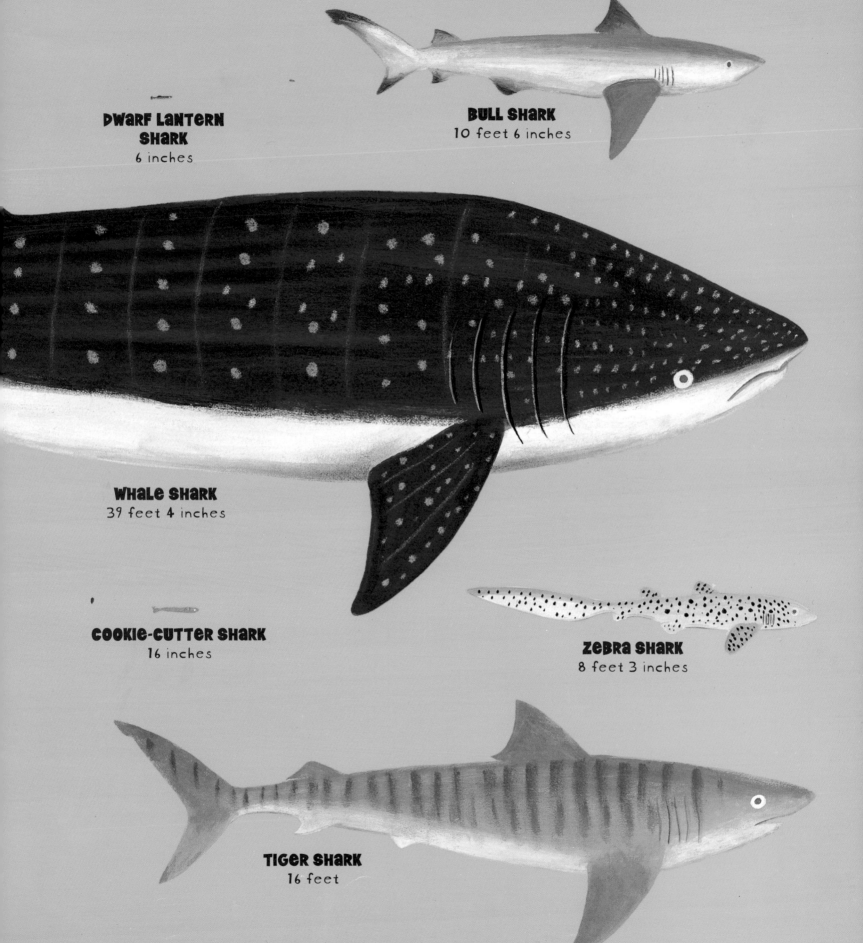

DWARF LANTERN SHARK
6 inches

BULL SHARK
10 feet 6 inches

WHALE SHARK
39 feet 4 inches

COOKIE-CUTTER SHARK
16 inches

ZEBRA SHARK
8 feet 3 inches

TIGER SHARK
16 feet

For the children of Hudson Primary
School, Sunderland
N. D.

For Mum, Dad, Lisa, and Wayne
J. C.

First U.S. paperback edition with CD 2008
The Library of Congress has cataloged the hardcover edition as follows:

Davies, Nicola.

Surprising sharks / Nicola Davies ; illustrated by James Croft — 1st U.S. ed.
p. cm.
Summary: Introduces many different species of sharks, pointing out such
characteristics as the small size of the dwarf lantern shark and the physical
characteristics and behavior that make sharks killing machines.
ISBN 978-0-7636-2185-8 (hardcover)
1. Sharks —Juvenile literature. [1. Sharks.] I. Croft, James, date, ill.
II. Title
QL638.9D426 2003
597.3 — dc21   2003040943

ISBN 978-0-7636-2742-3 (paperback)
ISBN 978-0-7636-3837-5 (paperback with CD)

2 3 4 5 6 7 8 9 10

Printed in China

This book was typeset in Blockhead and Sitcom.
The illustrations were done in acrylic and pastel.

Candlewick Press
2067 Massachusetts Avenue
Cambridge, Massachusetts 02140

visit us at www.candlewick.com

SURPRISING SHARKS

Nicola Davies

illustrated by
James Croft

CANDLEWICK PRESS
CAMBRIDGE, MASSACHUSETTS

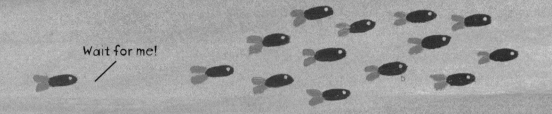

Wait for me!

You're swimming in the warm blue sea.
What's the one word that turns your
dream into a nightmare?
What's the one word that
makes you think of a
giant
man-eating
killer?

Shark? Yes, it's a shark!

It's a **DWARF LANTERN SHARK**.
It's the smallest kind of shark in the world,
just bigger than a chocolate bar. Not a giant,
certainly no man-eater, and a killer only
if you happen to be a shrimp.

You see, MOST sharks are not at all what you might expect. After all, who would expect a shark to . . .

Like all LANTERN SHARKS, this BLACKBELLY LANTERN SHARK has light-making organs on its tummy. They help it to blend in with the silvery surface of the sea and avoid ending up as dinner for bigger fish.

have built-in fairy lights . . .

or blow up like a party balloon . . .

SWELL SHARKS swallow water when they get scared. They blow up to three times their normal size so that they stick fast between rocks. Then no predator can pull them out.

This Australian shark is called a **WOBBEGONG**. Its patterned skin matches the rocks and coral on the sea floor, so it can sneak up on shellfish, crabs, and small fish without being seen.

or lie on the sea floor like a scrap of old carpet . . .

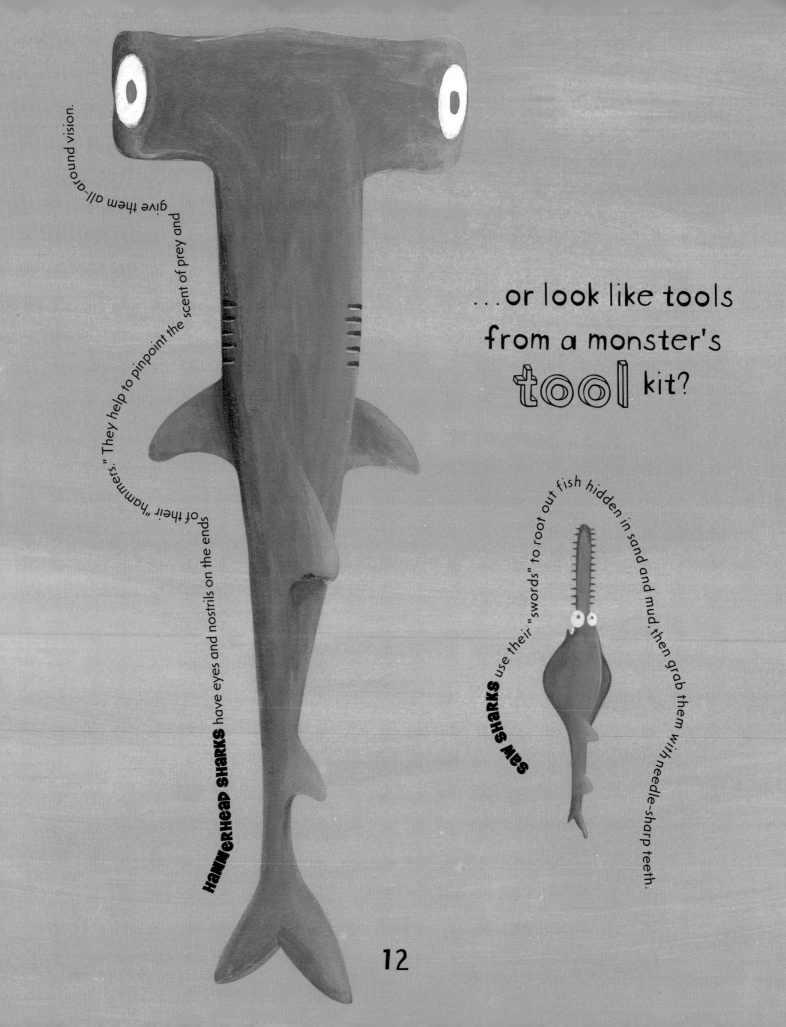

...or look like tools from a monster's **tool** kit?

HAMMERHEAD SHARKS have eyes and nostrils on the ends of their "hammers." They help to pinpoint the scent of prey and give them all-around vision.

SAW SHARKS use their "swords" to root out fish hidden in sand and mud, then grab them with needle-sharp teeth.

12

In fact, sharks come in all sorts of
shapes and **sizes.**

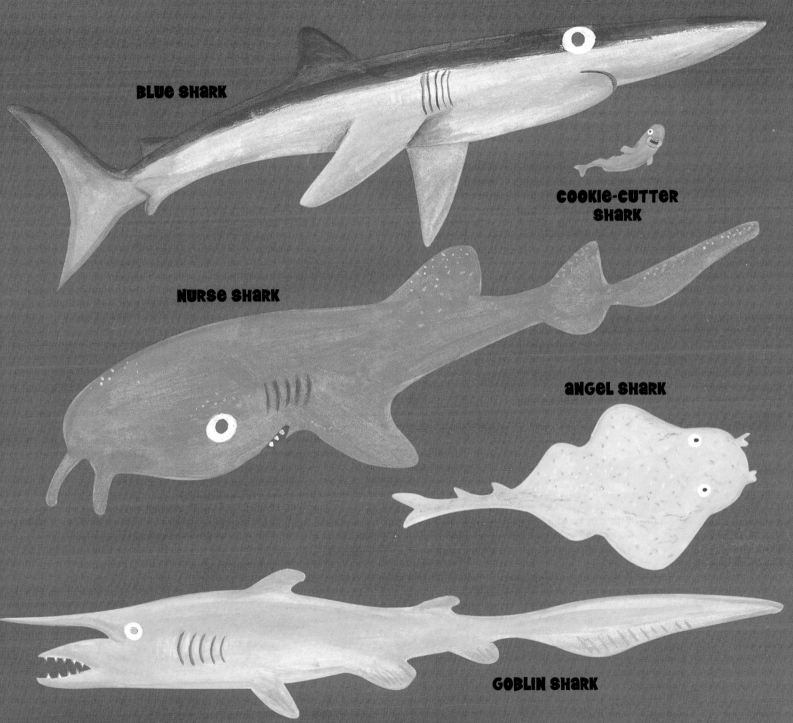

BLUE SHARK

COOKIE-CUTTER
SHARK

NURSE SHARK

ANGEL SHARK

GOBLIN SHARK

How can such different animals all be sharks?
Look carefully and you'll see
all the things they share.

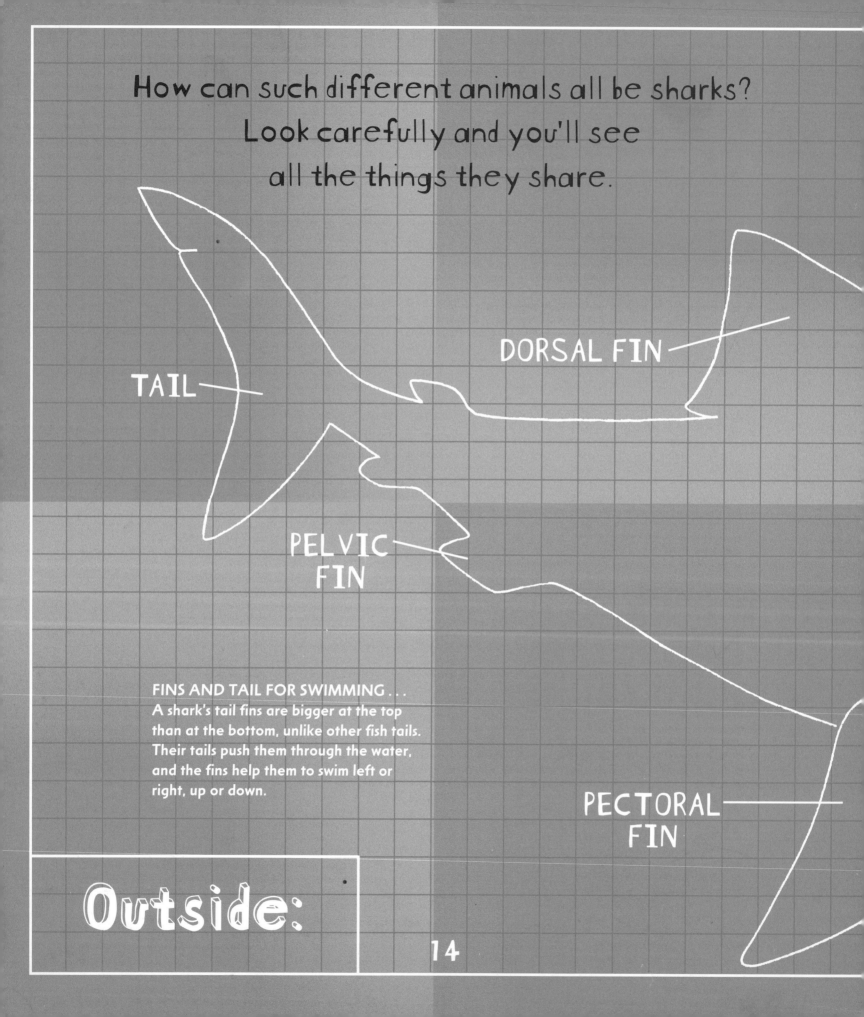

DORSAL FIN

TAIL

PELVIC FIN

FINS AND TAIL FOR SWIMMING . . .
A shark's tail fins are bigger at the top
than at the bottom, unlike other fish tails.
Their tails push them through the water,
and the fins help them to swim left or
right, up or down.

PECTORAL FIN

Outside:

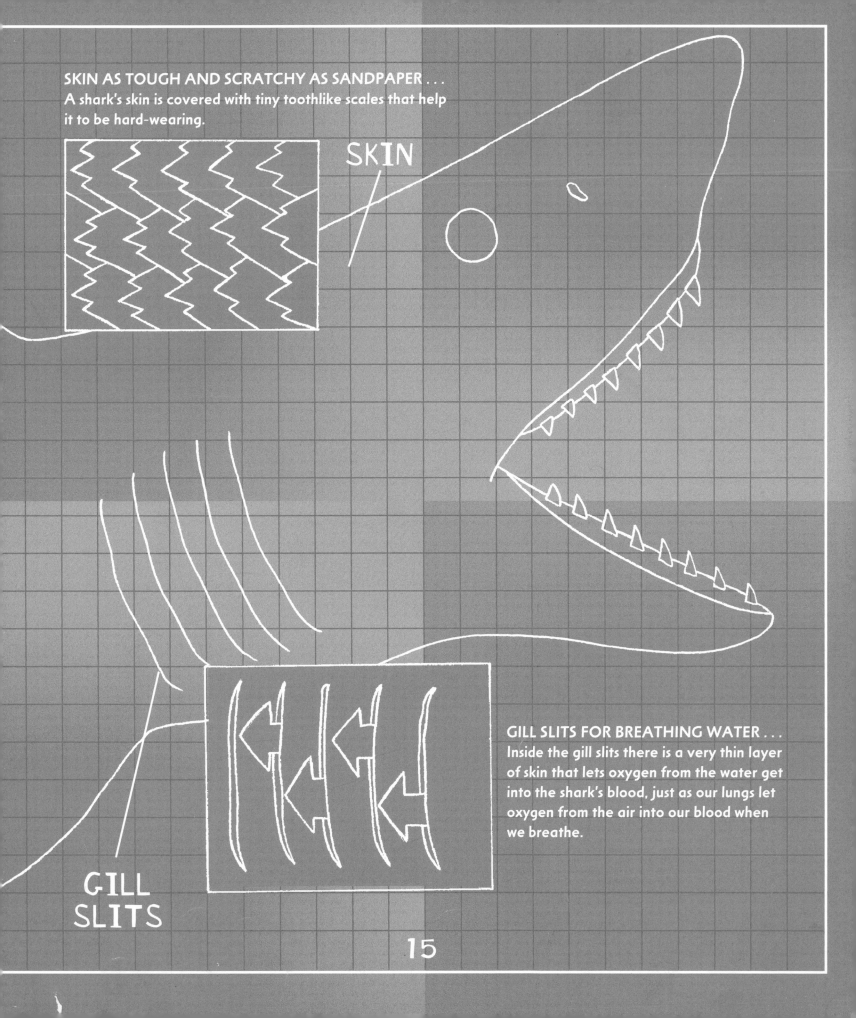

SKIN AS TOUGH AND SCRATCHY AS SANDPAPER . . .
A shark's skin is covered with tiny toothlike scales that help it to be hard-wearing.

SKIN

GILL SLITS FOR BREATHING WATER . . .
Inside the gill slits there is a very thin layer of skin that lets oxygen from the water get into the shark's blood, just as our lungs let oxygen from the air into our blood when we breathe.

GILL SLITS

Inside:

JAWS THAT CAN POP OUT THROUGH THE MOUTH, LIKE A JACK-IN-THE-BOX...
Sharks' jaws aren't part of their heads as ours are. Instead, they're held on by a kind of living rubber band, so the jaws can shoot forward fast to grab prey.

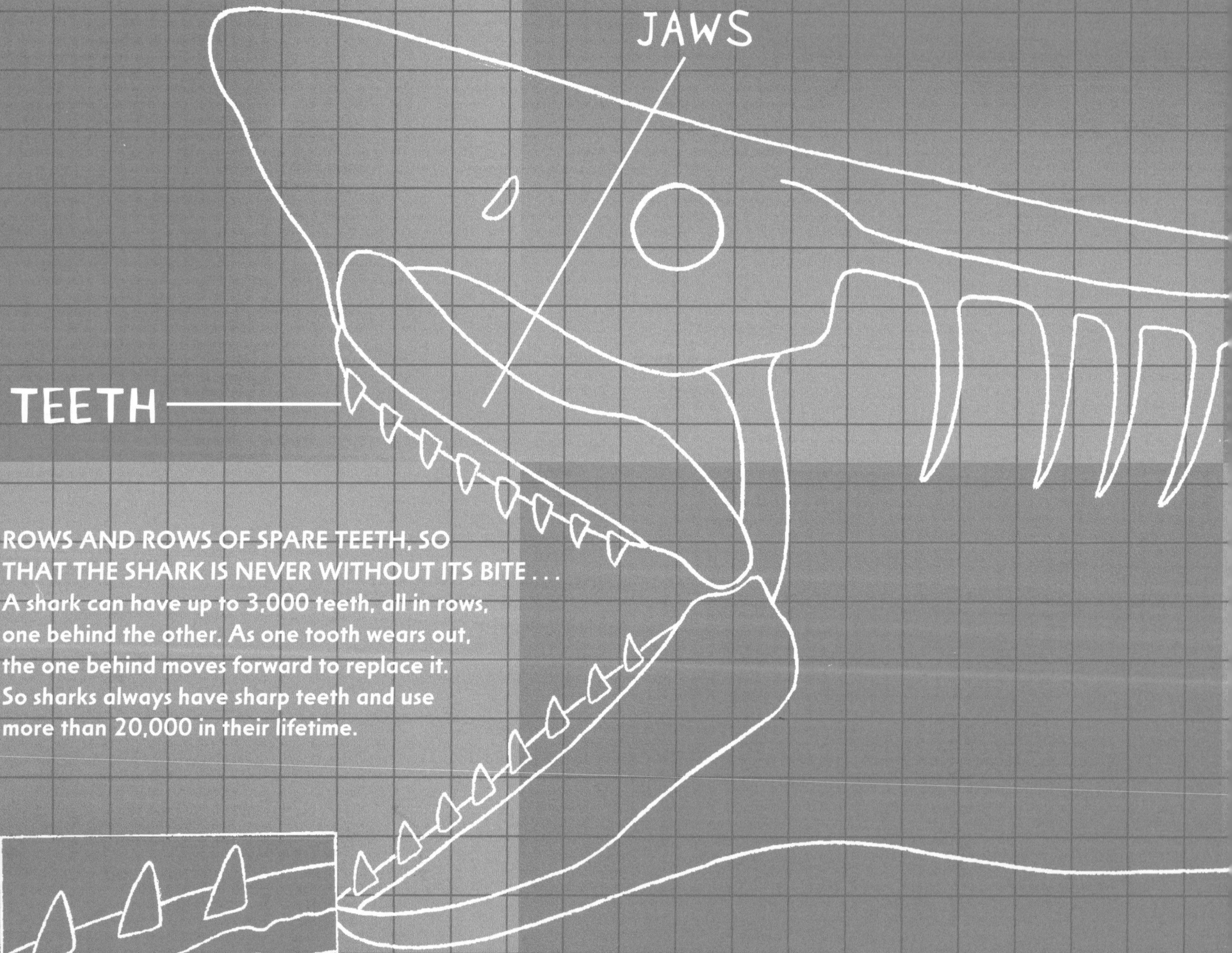

JAWS

TEETH

ROWS AND ROWS OF SPARE TEETH, SO THAT THE SHARK IS NEVER WITHOUT ITS BITE...
A shark can have up to 3,000 teeth, all in rows, one behind the other. As one tooth wears out, the one behind moves forward to replace it. So sharks always have sharp teeth and use more than 20,000 in their lifetime.

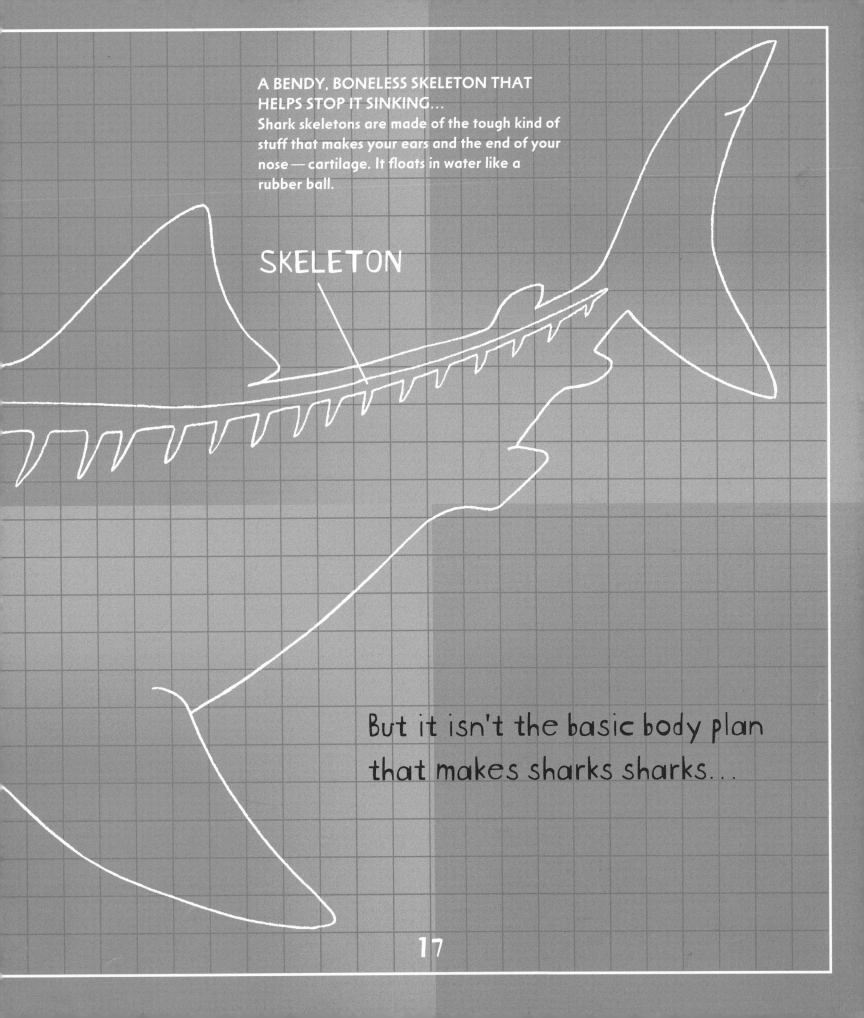

A BENDY, BONELESS SKELETON THAT HELPS STOP IT SINKING...
Shark skeletons are made of the tough kind of stuff that makes your ears and the end of your nose — cartilage. It floats in water like a rubber ball.

SKELETON

But it isn't the basic body plan that makes sharks sharks...

It's the **sharkish** way they behave!
Sharks are always hungry, and they're
always on the lookout for their next
meal. Some even start **killing**
before they're born.

SAND TIGER SHARKS
give birth to just two
live young—which is all
that's left after those two
have eaten the other six
babies in their mother's belly.

Let's get him!

Some sharks lay eggs, and some give birth to live
young. But all baby sharks are just like their
parents, with **sharp teeth** and
the ability to hunt right from the start.

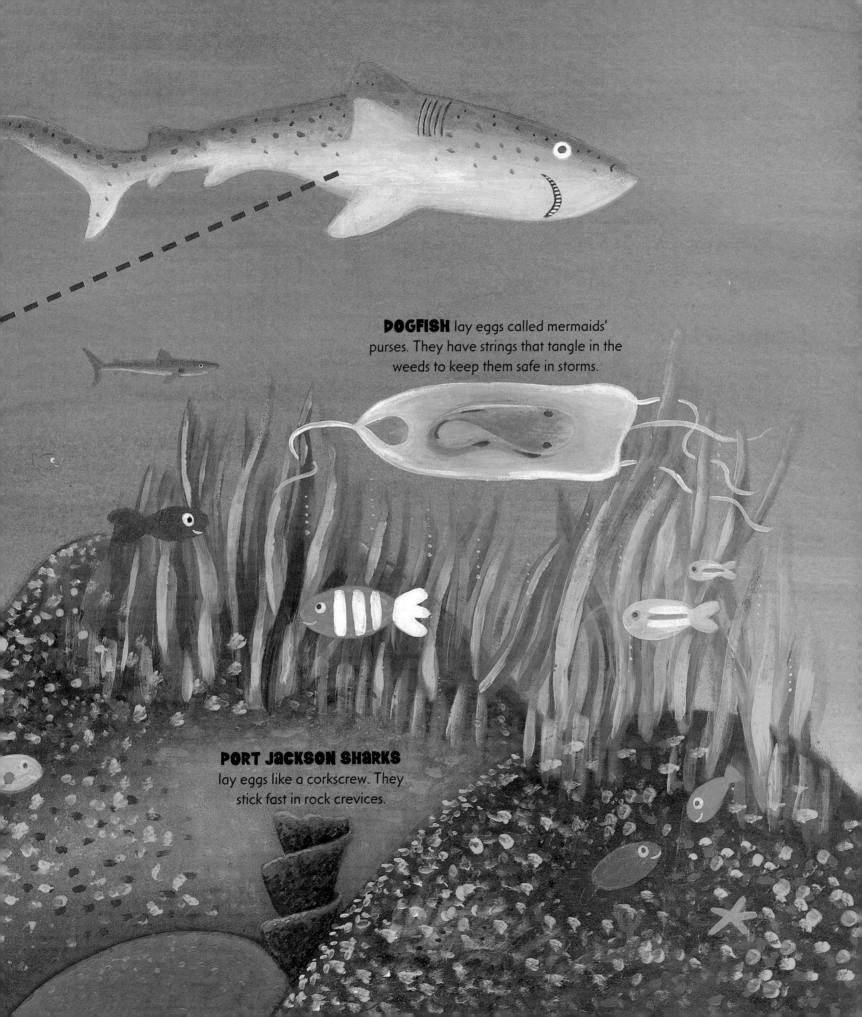

DOGFISH lay eggs called mermaids' purses. They have strings that tangle in the weeds to keep them safe in storms.

PORT JACKSON SHARKS lay eggs like a corkscrew. They stick fast in rock crevices.

Sharks' senses are fine-tuned, ready for the tiniest hint that might mean **food**!

Sharks have tiny holes to let sound into their inner ears. They can hear sounds that are too low for our ears to pick up.

Sharks' eyes are on the sides of their heads, so they can see almost as well behind them as they can in front!

The whole of a shark's skin is sensitive in the same way that your fingertips are. You can tell hot from cold, rough from smooth, moving from still. A shark can also get all sorts of information from the movement and temperature of the water all around its body.

To a hungry shark, the faintest trail of clues
is as clear as a restaurant sign.

A shark's nostrils are just under the
tip of its snout. Water flows into
them as the shark moves forward,
bringing any scents with it.

Gel-filled pits in a shark's
nose can detect food. Every
animal has nerves, which are
like cables carrying electrical
messages around the body.
The shark's gel pits can sense
this electricity.

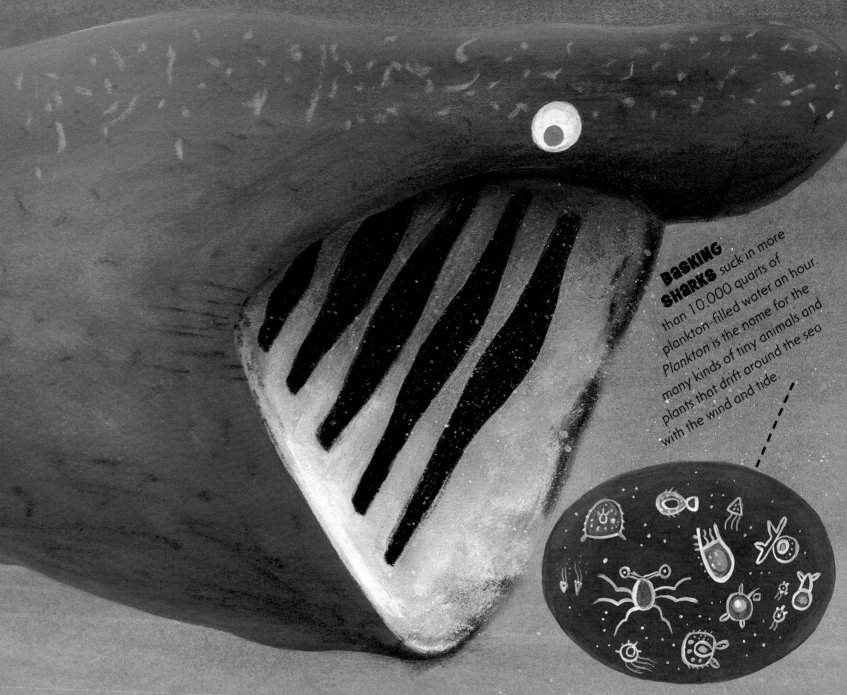

BASKING SHARKS suck in more than 10,000 quarts of plankton-filled water an hour. Plankton is the name for the many kinds of tiny animals and plants that drift around the sea with the wind and tide.

And when at last they're close enough for the kill, they feel the **crackle** of their prey's living nerves, so they bite in just the right place . . . no matter what the prey! Whether it's **plankton** . . .

or **people**! Oh yes, it's true — some sharks do kill people, about six of us every year.

The **GREAT WHITE** is one of just three species of sharks that attack people regularly. The other two are the **BULL SHARK** and the **TIGER SHARK**. In fact, only 30 of the 500 different kinds of sharks have ever attacked humans. Crocodiles, elephants, dogs, and even pigs kill more people every year than sharks do!

But every year **people** kill 100 million sharks.

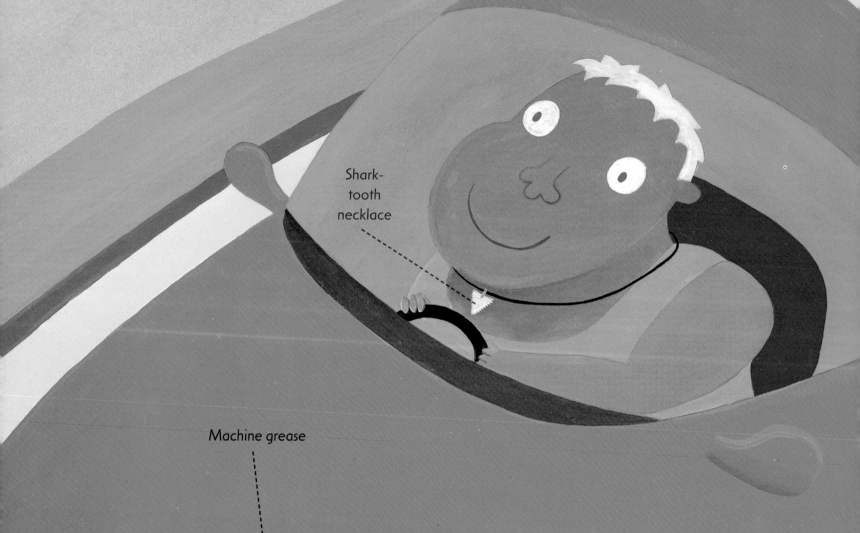

Shark-
tooth
necklace

Machine grease

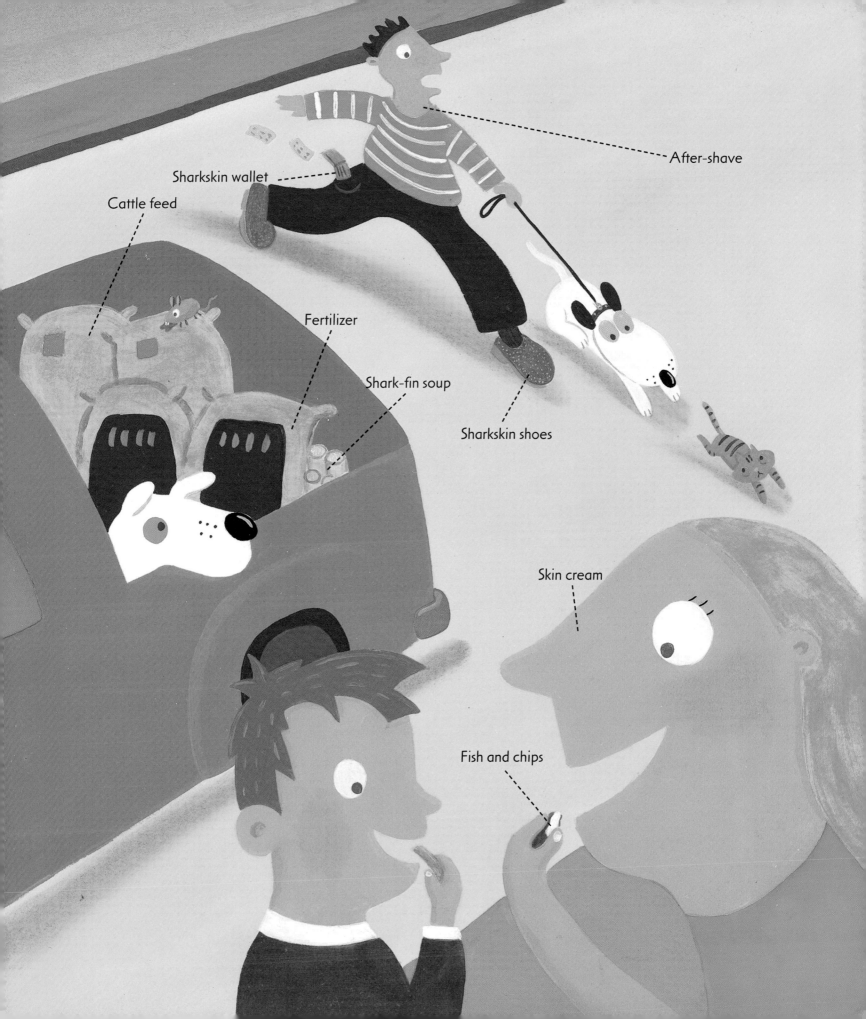

After-shave

Sharkskin wallet

Cattle feed

Fertilizer

Shark-fin soup

Sharkskin shoes

Skin cream

Fish and chips

If you were a shark swimming in the lovely blue sea, the last word you'd want to hear would be . . .

HUMAN!

Index

Look up the pages to find out about all these shark things. Don't forget to look at both kinds of words — this kind and this kind.

about Sharks

Sharks have been on Earth for 300 million years and can be found today in every ocean and sea in the world. People see sharks as monsters, but of the 500 different kinds of sharks in the world, only 30 have ever attacked humans, and most feed on shellfish and small fishes.

Sharks are predators: they kill only to eat and are as important in the sea as wolves, lions, tigers, and bears are on land.

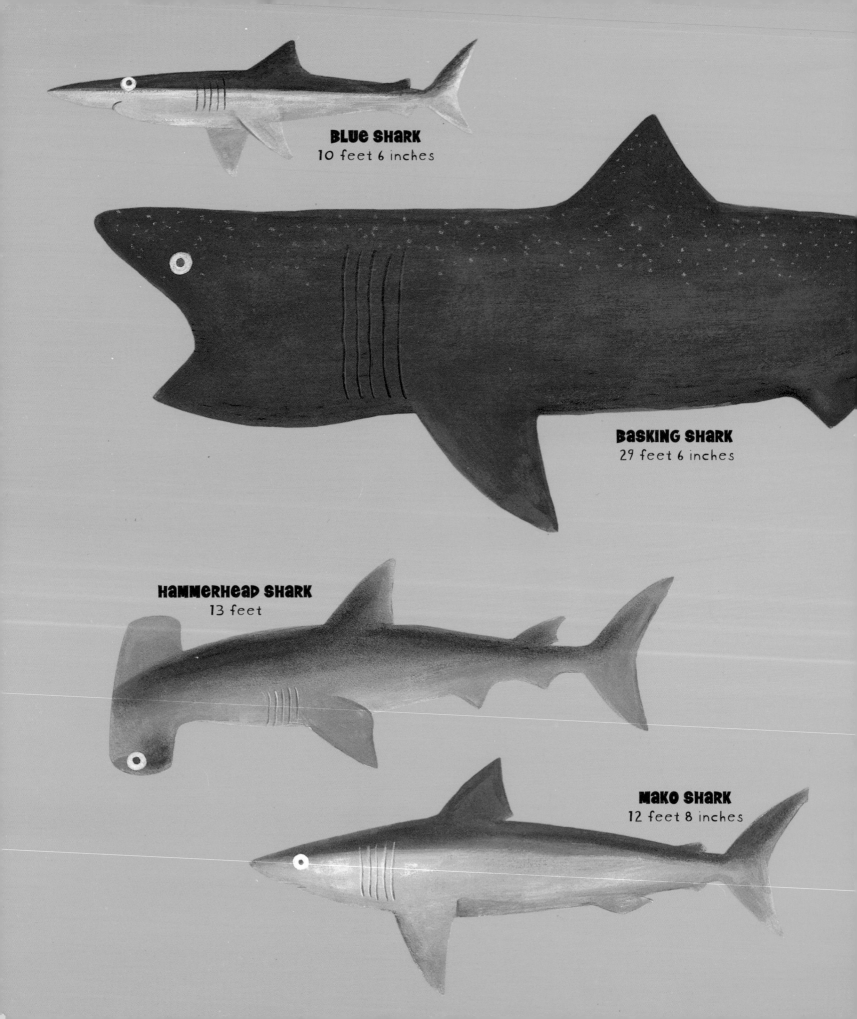

BLUE SHARK
10 feet 6 inches

BASKING SHARK
29 feet 6 inches

HAMMERHEAD SHARK
13 feet

MAKO SHARK
12 feet 8 inches

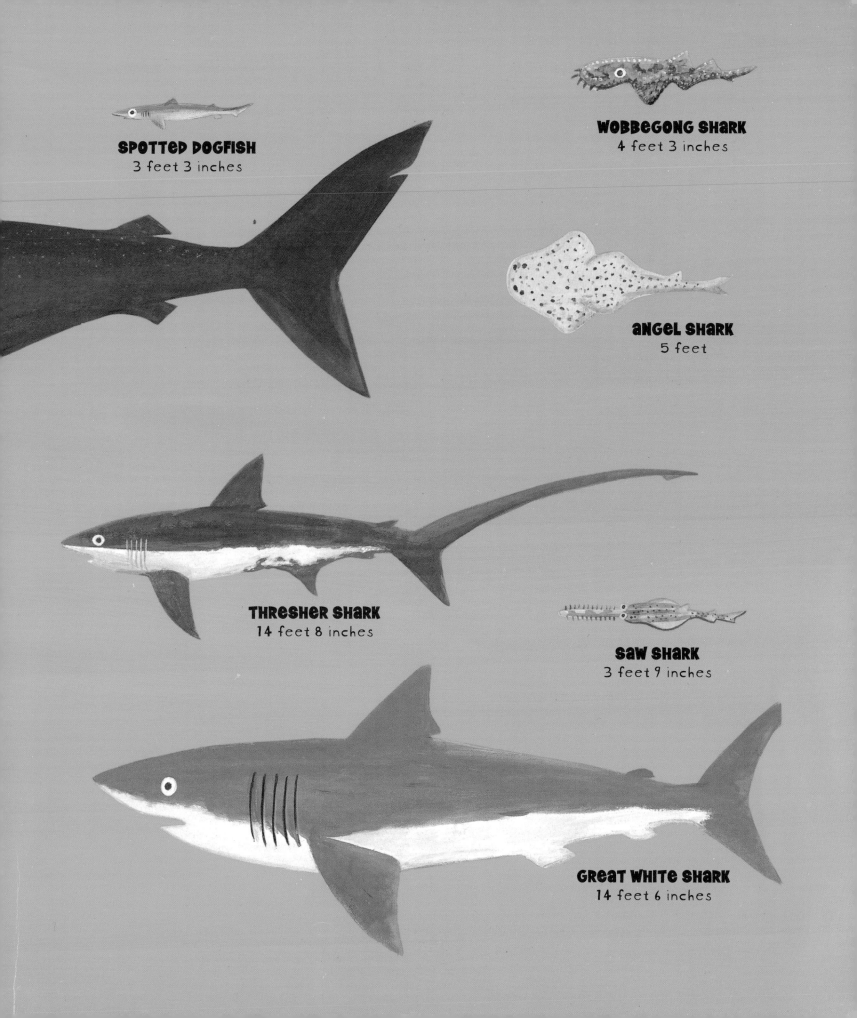

SPOTTED DOGFISH
3 feet 3 inches

WOBBEGONG SHARK
4 feet 3 inches

ANGEL SHARK
5 feet

THRESHER SHARK
14 feet 8 inches

SAW SHARK
3 feet 9 inches

GREAT WHITE SHARK
14 feet 6 inches

NICOLA DAVIES, a zoologist and author of such books as *One Tiny Turtle*, *Bat Loves the Night*, and *Extreme Animals: The Toughest Creatures on Earth*, has a special love for the sea. She has seen basking sharks off the coast of England and once came face-to-face with a shark while she was snorkeling—a baby spotted dogfish about the size of a sardine. Since sharks have been on Earth a lot longer than humans, she feels they deserve our respect and protection.

JAMES CROFT has always enjoyed drawing sharks and finds that their teeth and their speed, as well as the sense of danger they evoke, fuel his imagination like no other creature. He is the illustrator of numerous books for children, including the Brand New Readers *Mouse Has Fun* and *Mouse Goes Out* by Phyllis Root.